To Touch a Heart
Annalee Schade

To Touch a Heart
Annalee Schade

Copyright © 2023 by Austin Mardon
All rights reserved. This book or any portion thereof may not be reproduced or used in any manner whatsoever without the express written permission of the publisher except for the use of a brief quotations in a book review or scholarly journal.
First Printing: 2023

Typeset and Cover Design by Annalee Schade

ISBN: 978-1-77889-063-5

Golden Meteorite Press
103 11919 82 ST NW
Edmonton, AB T5B 2W3
www.goldenmeteoritepress.com

Preface

This book is a compilation of poems that I wrote throughout my highschool years. Most of the poems I wrote as a way of getting my thoughts organized, to try and come up with an answer to a question, or as a way to express myself. The poems were also a way to get people thinking. Some of these poems were more personal, trying to use words to express a feeling. The majority of them were me just trying to explore thoughts, concepts, and imagery.

I decided to get my poems published as a way to touch people's hearts. To inspire others like me, young authors, and those who struggle with mental disabilities, learning disabilities, or both. It can feel daunting to try something that you dream of doing when it feels like you are steps behind everyone else. I hope this book can be an inspiration for at least one person to feel like they can achieve their dream or calling. This is not a book about dreams, this book is the achievement of a dream.

Introduction

To Touch a Heart

One of the great privileges of being a teacher is not only getting to meet wonderful people who happen to be your students, but also to get a glimpse into their minds and to play a role (though a much smaller role than they give you credit for) in helping them discover, and prepare to fulfill,
their mission in life. For me, one such student was Annalee Schade. The glimpse into her mind that I saw in her work, and in her poetry, made me want to do whatever I could to help her share her perspectives with the world. Again, this is an important job of a teacher: To help your students see where they could go and ever so gently push them towards that destination.

Annalee and I have something in common: We are both on the autism spectrum. I have written about this a little in the introduction to my compilation of articles, stories, and poetry, Spitting Towards the West: Catholic Ruminations from the Edge of the Autism Spectrum (also published by Golden Meteorite Press, a wonderful outlet for giving neurodivergent people a voice). That book was one autist's perspective; perhaps this one will give you another. The more we can share each other's worlds, the richer our shared world will be.

It may surprise some that someone with autism may be drawn to poetry. After all, isn't poetry imaginative and metaphorical and intuitive, while autism tends to make a person more literal, rational, and analytical? But, in fact, poetry is often at its most striking when it describes a common experience in literal language. To describe things as they actually are is so rare that such descriptions have the quality of a dramatic, revelatory epiphany. Consider a popular example from another American Catholic poet, Joyce Kilmer:

I think that I shall never see
A poem lovely as a tree.
A tree whose hungry mouth is prest
Against the earth's sweet flowing breast;

This is a reference to trees absorbing nutrients from the soil into which their roots have sunk. But the phrase "absorbing nutrients" creates no real mental image: It is vague, misty, almost mystical, and the "scientific" terminology of mycorrhizal symbiosis is even less concrete. The autistic mind grasps on the solid and literal, and what is literally happening is that the tree is eating its food in the form of sucking a kind of nourishing fluid from the earth. The hole through which we receive our nourishment is typically called a mouth; the way trees eat, when described literally, sounds rather like a nursing baby on the breast of Mother Earth. This is poetic, and perhaps "metaphorical," but it only works because it is so very literal. Compare this to Ms. Scade's lines:

Every day leaves battle the wind,
A battle for survival,
A war they know they lose.

Is this a metaphor or is it literal? It is both; it is poetry.

The autistic mind is certainly analytical, but this, too, is totally consonant with poetry. Academics doing qualitative research often do "coding" of their interview transcripts in which they pick out key phrases the participants have used. Johnny Saldana notes that this can actually form a kind of "found poetry." If you ever make notes in the margins of your books, you may discover, upon isolating them from the text you are annotating, that you have accidentally written free verse poetry.

Ms. Schade does this as well; the character of Lady Macbeth sticks in her mind and whirls around, thoughts sticking to her as she spins until, like cotton candy, those images and reflections have accumulated into a vivid description of her. Other shining imaginative digressions trail behind the flying sparks of random thoughts: The band name "Boyz II Men" inspires a reflection in verse on the process of masculine maturity. An autistic mind may work in a linear fashion, but those lines of thought work outwards from stray, disparate, floating musings.

In a conversation with William F. Buckley, Jr. on Firing Line, the poet Jorge Luis Borges remarked:

MR. BORGES: "Art happens," [Whistler] said. And I think that's true. I should say that beauty happens. Sometimes I think that beauty is not something rare. I think beauty is happening all the time. Art is happening all the time. At some conversation a man may say a very fine thing, not being aware of it. I am hearing fine sentences all the time from the man in the street, for example. From anybody.

MR. BUCKLEY: So you consider yourself a transcriber, to a certain extent.

MR. BORGES: Yes, in a sense I do, and I think that I have written some fine lines, of course.

Everybody has written some fine lines.

You will find Ms. Schade some fine lines in the pages within.

Brett Fawcett
July 7, 2023

Life and Death

Blood Spilled, Soaked in love.
Sword swung down, Stayed by love's shield.
Father's arms that never hold, Female's child's hand.
Reddened blood cleaner, Squealing baby.
Mother's child hewn down, Children's toys give way,
Shields hide sensitive eyes, Slowly not children grow.
Arrows fly higher still, Armor and shields,
Hearts torn out, Held by loved ones.
Pyres burn on the horizon, Picked wreaths of lilies.
Silence and darkness, Shields of white,
Shadows lurking, Splinter the dark with light.
Darkness no where near, Darlings home,
Splintered guardian not needed In the splendor.

Needle of Silver

Why do you hurt so much?
Crimson blood, crimson thread,
Background of white,
A canvas for pain.
Screams like birds burst forth,
Snow like cold razors,
Coming down, turning the very earth cold.
The pain of a Queen.
Life given in the cold,
Life taken by the cold.
Desolate cry of a child
Hair as black as raven,
Lips the color of silver pain,
Skin the color of stole a mother.

The child grows in stature and beauty,
Cold as the thing she is called after,
Snow.

Tongue as sharp as icicles
And just as cold.
A heart as of ice,
Far she thinks from God's heat.

Men from far and wide come,
Trying to claim her icy heart.
Scorning all, she lives in her shell,
Thinking she is beyond love.

Sitting alone in her palace of frost,
A man His clothes are soiled and carrying a bundle
Comes before her.
Inquiring His business His answer is peculiar,
Asking after a lamb that is lost,
No sheep was there, and what of the bundle?
A gift for a heart,
Beckoned, He approaches,
A white unlike snow was the cloth
Nails, thorns, and a head of a spear
These are what?
I use to offer Myself,
For what?
For you.

Fire spread, white and warm from Him,
Arrows pierced that heart of ice,
Crevices crack through icy walls.

Her shell of ice broke open.
Stepping between the cracks,
Who is He?

She stood trembling,
I am.
Ice crashing down,
Arms encircling,
Safe and warm,
Filling cracks not of ice,
Of heart.

Mother by a Pond

Sun on a silver pond,
Shines on a mother fond.
Sitting among flowers blue
People see her few.
Flowers crown her head,
A queen it has been said,
Wrapped in gold and silver,
Twelve starts not slivers
Like a cosmo surround.
No one her could hound,
Request she grants,
Helper on quests.
She bore a King,
To whom Angels sing.
From battle not she shies,
All life dies,
Who she favors, survives
But not for own lives,
For He who has risen.

Boys to Men

How can you tell when a boy turns into a man?
Is it through experience?
Or learning they had childhood sense?
Could it be the actions they take?
Maturity?
Fluency?
Are these the attributes that make boys men?
Wisdom?
Freedom?
How do these affect boys to men?
Success?
Generous?
Where is the line from boys to men?
By ritual?
Or is it physical?
Boyhood turning to manhood?
Do we decide?
Or is it for God to decide?
When boys become men.

Jewels and Gold

Blood red as rubies.
Caught in golden chalice,
Bestowed upon us earthly beings.
A crown studded with rubies and sapphires.
Water the color sapphires rains down,
Soaking the earth and giving plenty.
People wage war,
But on high conquers
And holds the crown.

Meet Me Where I Am At

Meet me where I am at,
For it is only with you I move forward.
On my own I only move back,
Step by step, day by day I never stay the same.
The face I see in the mirror is different every day.
How can anyone get to know me,
When I am still getting to know myself?
You are the one who holds the answers,
The key,
And the lock.

The Battle of the Leaf

Every day leaves battle the wind,
A battle for survival,
A war they know they lose.
Day in and out, they fight for their place.
Spring and summer when warm winds blow,
The leaves hold their ground.
Then around autumn comes,
And they show their dying colors.
Ice, frost and snow the battle is lost.
To be taken up again with new fervor come spring.
Only to be lost again.
But still leaves fight for where they belong,
Though all is doomed.

Mustard Seed

Lift the veil from my eyes,
Rend it in two,
All the embroidery destroy,
The costly fabric and jewels fall to the floor
They pale in comparison.
Stitch by careful stitch unravel it,
For realty it shrouds.

Rubies and diamonds carved like roses adorn.
A path straight and narrow,
A throne made of olive branches,
A scale at His feet.
Two angels, one holds a crook and the other a whip
The third stands alone.

A heart hard and heavy with more than a few cracks,
Stands before Him.
In a place with hearts like gardens,
This heart is like a stone.

A woman steps forward, wrapped in the sky,
She takes the heart and wipes away the dust,
And in that heart is a tiny sprig,
A sprig from a mustard seed.

She gives the heart to her son,
"This is a heart that can move mountains,
I have seen hearts boasting gardens
That could not tell a tree to move a branch."

The man took the heart,
Broke away the rock to reveal the roots.
Then He filled in the cracks and holes with gold.
"Welcome to paradise."

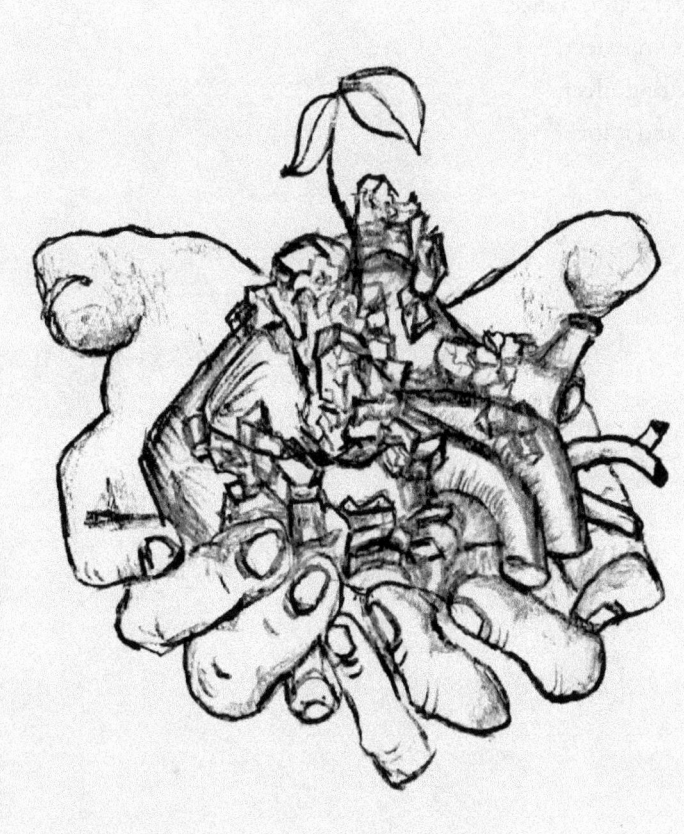

Unity Or Uniformity?

Unity or uniformity?
Which will make us happy?
Both lack conflict.
To be who we are and our path,
Or what is demanded in a path well traveled?
An identity to be discovered through trial,
Or an identity given to everyone and no one?
Which is more true?
Which is real peace?
One is only the appearance,
The other is imperfect,
But has a lasting effect.
Which has and is love?

Thoughtless Love

You envelope us in Your love,
We harm you unknowingly.
We come running,
You forgive,
But we turn and run again
And You still love.
This is our weakness,
That is Your strength,
To love without a thought
In good,
In bad,
You are there
Arms open,
Only to close around us.
We resist and we fight,
But you hold tight.
In our sorrow and shame,
You do not leave.
In Your pain and suffering,
We do not hear You.
The pain we cause,
We do not see.
Help us to see,
Help us to hear,
Guide our feet,
That we may come running
And never leave.

Mother

A lady of many titles,
She who has one job,
To be a mother.
To guard and protect,
To guide and comfort,
Her children,
The world.
No one denied,
No one turned down,
By the mother of all.
She marches off to war,
With them, her children.

The Want to be Noticed But The Fear of Being Seen

The outside is calm and collected.
But inside?
A voice is screaming out,
"Can you see me,
Will you notice me?"

We are talented,
But fear holds us back.
We want to share it with the world,
But also terrified.
Terrified of not being noticed,
Of not being loved.

Fear of them seeing too deep,
Of them seeing what we see,
What we think about ourselves,
Who we think we really are,
Failures and specks of dust.

We stay where we are,
Not stepping out of our boundaries,
Where it is comfortable,
Where we think it is safe.

The walls seem to close in,
The fear does nothing but grow.
Our walls become so break,
It becomes crippling to think too.

You give us the hammer to do so,
And lend us the strength.
We may seem like specks of dust,
To You that dust is gold.
We may still fear,
But we do not cower.

Value

What has the most value?
A stranger's smile?
A million dollars?
Which is better?
To give someone soup,
Or buy a diamond?
Who has more power?
One who gives?
The one who takes?
We only have one life.
How are you going to live it,
In greed and misery?
In loneliness and fear?
Or in going out
To do good,
To make smiles,
To show people the path,
The path to God.

The Forgotten Dark

People forget what the dark is like,
In the light they take for granted.
They can let their brightness fade,
And not know it is happening.
People in dark know not the light,
They have forgotten what it is like.
When a spark comes, they may fear the light,
They attack it try to tear it to shreds,
But the light does not go out.
They may follow it or stay,
Stay in what they know,
Stay in the dark cage.
Or they may follow the path,
Find the gate,
To the One who knows their name.
They never forget the dark,
But they cannot go back.
There is more light than dark.
As Light can reignite and scatter the gloom,
It can also fade,
But You are there with Your rod and Your staff
To guide us home,
Where we have a place.

Which Path to Take?

To whom should we turn, Oh, God?
For all is just sand if not thy rock.
There would be nothing for our anchors to hold,
Sand blown and washed away.
Its paths are hilly,
Those who traverse it sink among the grains.
Thy path is straight, narrow and lacks hills and valleys.
Who is their guide?
The followers of sand follow the blown dirt.
Thou hath provided map and compass,
Guide and supplies You bestow on us.
Thy path is straight and narrow, easy to walk,
But hard to choose.
The sand is alluring with jewels and scenery.
Thou hast given us beauty we do not comprehend.
We follow sand though it blows where the wind wills,
And the sand stings, we notice it not,
Until it grinds us down to what You formed us from.
We turn from that path and we follow you, Oh, God.

Lady McBeth

Gold Filigree,
Obsidian lace,
Fingers bedecked in blood.
Skirts of silk,
Eyes full of murder,
Handle towards her husband's hand.
Water clear and clean,
Her hands still soiled.
One once loyal and true,
Turn monstrous and cruel,
Clay solid in her hands.

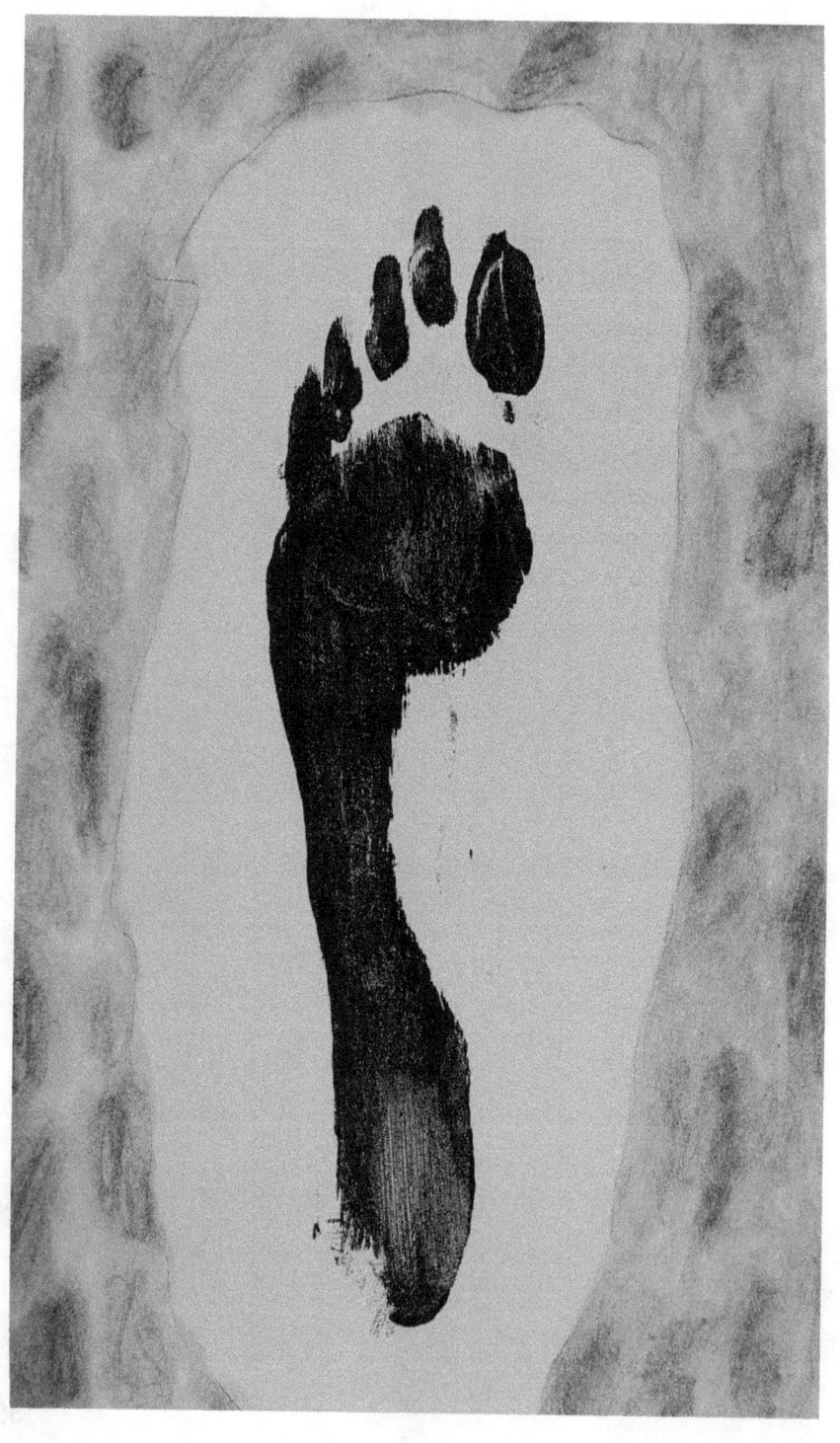

Those Feet of Jesus

Those feet of Jesus, taking their first step with Mary at Your side.
Those feet of Yours brought you to the temple where you stayed.
They brought You to the waters' edge and walked on water.
Those feet of Yours took you from town to town, bringing the good news.
Those feet of Yours that fell out from under you on the way of the cross.
They were nailed to the cross for all humanity.
Those feet of Yours hold you in front of the apostles.
Those feet of Yours stood on a cloud as you returned home,
And they will stand again when You come to bring us home.

Falling

Falling, Falling,
Caressed by darkness,
Possessive of things not theirs.
Sticking, Sticking,
Never letting go.
Grooming, Grooming,
To take more souls.
Savior, Savior,
Come to save.
Light, Light,
Burn the dark away.

The Gates Thrown Wide

The sky darkens,
The sun blotted out.
Animals quiet.
Trembling rocks roll with the earth,
Gravestones burst and open.
The shroud is torn.
The gates thrown wide.
He who comes, He who died.

Martyrs

Who fights?
Who dies?
Martyrs in Your eyes.
Lives given.
Dead to the world,
But living in You.
Perfectly happy,
Perfectly loved,
Up with You above.

Found

Something lost,
Something found.
The tears roll down,
For the person they found.
The three who pour gold into cracks.
He whose blood poured forth,
To fill our holes.
Him who has no limits,
The one who gave us
Our arms to take up.
The war we fight ends
When we rest in Him
Who establish victory.

Knot

Tie the tether,
Tie your demise.
Slip the knot,
Set you free.
Let it sink to the watery depths.
For past is past,
Now matters,
And future depends on the now.
For looking back is a murderous path.

Tombs

The barren will yield,
The cold will warm,
The sun will shine and crack stone.
Doors open,
Clouds will come,
Rain will wash away the dust.
Blood became salvation,
An execution turned sacrifice.
The earth shook,
The dead rose,
Tombs opened,
Tombs will open.
Earth and heaven pass away.
God saves.

How Shall We Call Thee?

How shall we call Thee?
What title should we use?
Lord and Savior,
God and Brother?
What should we call Thee,
Teacher,
Father?
Our situation decides?
For they are all acceptable.
Who is fit to call upon thee?
No one is not allowed,
For we all fall,
We get up.
We call and praise Thee
No matter the hour,
No matter the day.
You hear us,
You call us.

Jewel

What am I without You, Lord?
I am dust,
Dust scattered in the cyclone of time.
From dust I came,
To dust I return.
Without You,
I am a creature of dust,
Destined to be blown away.
With You,
Pressure is applied.
I am condensed and refined.
When the wind stops blowing,
And the dust stills,
You pull my jewel out of the powder.

Where Do We Belong?

Where do we belong?
With You, Oh, God.
Do whom do we belong?
To You, Oh, God.
Our salvation You gave us.
You bought it at a high cost,
Laying down Your life.
We do not deserve such love and loyalty,
But the gift shall not be turned away.
I bend my knee at Thy altar,
I eat Thy flesh and drink Thy blood.
Thy gift shall not be turned away.
You live in my heart,
I belong to You,
And I live in You.

Who Am I?

Who am I today?
Who am I tomorrow?
Who is consistent?
Only You, God, are consistent.
River of time rushes past,
Changing landscapes,
And minds are not immune.
The face you see in the mirror
Never appears twice.

Who Shall I Be?

Who am I now?
Who shall I be?
My thoughts are persistent,
My morals define,
My actions show through.
God, You gave me my morals,
My thoughts are my own,
Actions say what I mean,
Words are just a puff of air.
What is their meaning?
So easily confused.

The Silent Word

The Silent Word,
Quiet as a mountain,
Carving like a river.
Lives it shapes,
It's bestowed on us.

Gently the cross
It caresses,
It raises,
It implants in our hearts.

The Silent Word comes,
Wrapped in splendor
It descends,
Abundant as the dew drops,
Soaking into our hearts,
Bearing salvation.

Lay Down

Release,
Let go,
Lay down
Every burden and I will take it.
Burden,
Yoke,
Package,
Every one I will hold.
Heavy,
Crushing,
Suffocating
I will take it.
What are these in comparison
To the weight I bore at Calvary,
The price I paid for?
You bend,
And you break,
I will support you and hold that weight.

Path

Walking down a path,
It is lined with flowers.
Sharp stones caress
Bare feet that walk upon.
That path lined with silken petals.
A tomb ahead,
The outside lined with moss and ivy.
The stone is rolled to the side.
The inside,
The inside blooming,
Flowers of white lilies
Faced towards the Son.
And there He sits,
Head adorn with a crown of thorns.
Among the thorns are white and red roses,
From them dangle sapphire teardrops.
Standing from His throne,
Declaring He says,
"I have turned your shame,
To glory.
Your sadness,
To joy.
Take My hand
And walk upon the waters."

Overwhelmed

Swimming,
Swaying,
Swarming,
Spearing,
Somewhere,
Shouldn't be
Swirling,
Swerving,
Staying,
Starting,
Sounds,
Sounds,
Sounds,
Smothering,
Stop,
Just stop it,
Quiet,
Please.

Worth

What is my worth,
If not found in Thee, Oh, Lord?
Dust I would not be,
Not salt,
Nor tree,
Not anything would I be.
For in You value is found.
In You the price decided.
Am I worth emerald and pearls?
No!
Rubies, sapphires and diamonds,
That was the price.

Start

At the beginning, when I start,
When do I truly start?
Bright signs point this way and that,
Which one do I choose?
The plain wooden one with simple letters,
That is where I go.
It takes me one way,
Away, away from neon lights.
Then I see a light and follow that,
Deviating from the path.
Then I find another wooden sign.
Is this from where I start?
Following the path to the rising sun,
I get distracted by a gem off the path.
Picking it up I see it is nothing but sharpened glass.
Blood running down my fingers,
Back to the wooden path I go.
I start again,
Nothing but scars on my hand
And chains dragging behind.
A man comes and says,
"Let me take your chains."
I clutch them to my chest.
With a soft command He says,
"Let me, I will continue to ask."
I give up my chains.
He walks beside me
Pointing out small beautiful things.
He smiles saying,
"Start again, for when did you truly stop?"

Faith

How can I follow a path I cannot see?
I need to trust in You blindly.
Faith is what I need.
Is it given, found or gained?
I need to learn to trust Thee,
Especially when things seem contradicting.

A path I don't see,
A path I want to be following.
Will they cross?
Or will they not even touch?
I need faith.
But how do I gain it?
How do I use it?

You Clear the Way

When all is dark,
How will I see Thee?
When sin has left its mark,
How will I be truly clean?
For it is my mind that holds me back.
When Your light comes,
I see through incense thick.
Though You clear the way,
I fall for their trick.
Though You heal the wound,
Scars in my mind stick.
How do I let go?
You wait patiently as the clock goes tick,
Waiting for me to forgive the one who sinned.

Alive Yet Dead

Water flows above me,
Yet I do not drown.
I am alive yet dead.
I am saved, yet I suffer.
Water is flowing but it is wine.
The bread is made of grain,
But it is flesh.
There is a place set,
But some will not sit.
These seem like contradictions,
Yet go hand in hand,
In Your hands.

Shoes

Which shoes do my feet fit into?
Do they belong in sandals,
Or are loafers better?
Shall I run barefoot,
Or walk down in glass slippers?
Is it in heels I will strut,
Or in flats I shall dance?
Will I wear sneakers to the gala,
Or hiking in wedge heels?
Or could it be I am meant to wear boots?
Lord, you are my cobbler.
What shall I wear?

Holy Family

Mary, Mother Mine,
Wrap me in thy mantel,
Hide me in thine skirt,
Lay my head on thine bosom.
Protect me,
As you protected thy son on earth.

Joseph, my spiritual father,
Please build my crib,
Spread food on thy table,
Hold my hand and walk me down the aisle,
Build my boat,
Which God will set a lite.
Guard me,
As you guarded Christ on earth.

Jesus, brother of mine,
You hold my hand,
You carry my heavy burden,
You place a crown of flowers on my head,
You bath me in Thy river,
You guide me,
As you guided Your disciples.

Mary, Joseph, Jesus

Mary, wrap my head in thy mantle.
Place my head on thy bosom.
Jesus, pour cleansing water on my head,
Crown my head with lilies.
Joseph, pull the thorns out of my ears and eyes.
Mary and Joseph, pray over my head.
Jesus, Jesus, Jesus,
Wash through my head with your blood,
And cleanse my head with your flesh.

Guardian

God's Servant, my Guardian,
Wrap me in your wings,
Light God's path,
Point out my mistakes.
Never permit to enter the dark,
And never permit the dark to enter into me.
Lead me to God.
Hold God's lantern high.
God's name is forever on your lips,
Help his name to stay on mine.
Thank you God's Angel.

Tomb of My Heart

Oh tomb of my heart,
Will thou not be like glass?
Oh tomb of my heart,
Why are thou so enclosed?
Burst open and show Him.
Oh tomb of my heart,
Why dost you stand like stone
And not more like a river flowing?
Oh tomb of my heart,
Do they still stand guard
Preventing you from opening?
Oh tomb of my heart,
If I cannot take the handle, knock,
The door shall open.

Straight Path

How do I reach?
How do I follow?
It feels like I
Jump through hoops
To get to
You
Looking back...
Was the path always that straight?

Trees

Is my heart like the evergreen,
Timeless, timeless in its color?

Or is it like the maple,
Leaves changing in sin?

Do my leaves stay rooted
As the wind of change blows through?

Or are the leaves snatched away
Blown about in the cyclone?

Is my trunk thick and strong,
Nourished by heat, unbothered by cold?

Or is it skinny as a sapling,
Untested by cold in lukewarm autumn?

Precious Jewel

Reaching my hands out,
You clasp them.
My tears come flowing down,
You dry them.
My heart comes broken and aching,
You heal it.
You want it.
You cherish it.
You parade it around,
Like a precious jewel.
Though it may be one of many,
You Love it dearly.
You Love individually.

Arms, Wings, Path

I lay down my arms,
Of twigs and sharpened rocks,
And pick up yours,
Of steel and mahogany.
They are meant to fight,
Fight battles won.
They should not gather dust
Unused on a shelf, put away.

I have these wings
They're not just to fly,
But to be Your wings,
To shield and to protect
As You shield and protect.

You gave me a path,
Not just to walk along it.
You gave this path to guide.
I'm to walk and show.
Show you to others,
Walk with them to You,
Till paths diverge.

Sun Beam

A great tumultuous lake
Dark with storm clouds.
The waves rise and crash.
They batter against a rock
That rises above
Tall and strong
Piercing to the sky.
The rock brandishes
Brandishes a flower
Brandishes a lily.
The Sun drives through the clouds
Nurturing the lily.
The waves cannot reach,
The wind cannot batter.
The rock holds,
And the Sun nurtures.

I Am Death
I Am Life

Running

Why do they run to me?
Why do others shove them to me?
Their minds cause them to seek me,
But in me solace cannot be found.
Coming to me only makes the gavel come down.
He may be merciful,
But they condemn themselves.

Stay, oh stay until called,
See the beauty she holds.
See what has been given.
Oh how it pains me to hold a child.
How can you not clutch her hand and run to Him.
It pains me to see you cling to me.
I hold not beauty but for who I call.

I am Death

My Hands are Cold

My hands are cold,
Stay in warmth.
I cannot keep you,
Go where you can stay.
My home is suffering,
With Him is happiness.
I do not want you here,
He Loves you.

Can you not see,
I only bring pain.
I cannot bandage your scratches,
I only make them bleed.
Go to Him,
Do not look back.

I am Death

Why am I Here?

Why am I here?
Why did I come to be?
Suffering is what I bring.
Why was that fruit eaten?

"They had a choice.
You are Death, so there might be life.
Through you life can be gained,
Through your defeat they are forgiven.
They may stay with you,
But you exist for Life.

You are Death."

Graveyards

I walk through graveyards,
Seeking those who do not stay.
Oh Death, you keep so many,
I wish it was not so.
I cling to them but they let go.
As much as I try
To hold them,
To keep them,
They run and hide.
They hide in Death,
They cling to the shadows.
Oh how I wish to bring them,
Bring them to God
And keep them with me,
With Him.

I am Life

Oh Death

Oh Death,
How you cling to my skirts,
Taking what you are given,
And passing them along.
Some cling to you like burrs.
Oh how I wish to clean you,
And take those who are suffering.
But they are yours,
For they chose you.
You do not want them,
But they are there.
I wish to keep them
And pass them on myself,
But that is selfish of me.

I am Life

Grave

How grass grows on a grave,
How fires burn dead foliage,
How rotting trees nurture.
There was once Life without Death
They now live because they die
And they die because they live.
You are Life,
You are Death,
You walk hand in hand.

Do Not Misunderstand

Do not misunderstand,
I will not let you go.
I may mourn and cry,
But I will call you,
As a Siren who sings,
You cannot escape.
From the garden,
To the Cross,
I hang over your shoulder.
He dictates the song
But I am coming,
Until He comes.

I am Death

Authors Bio

Annalee Schade was born in Indiana then at a young age moved to Illinois, during her Junior year of High School her family moved back to Indiana. She personally had to work through Dyslexia and having a writing disorder. Having Autism allows her to view the world in a different light. She was diagnosed with Dyslexia a year before starting high school and with being on the Autism Spectrum in her Sophomore year. She was Homeschooled up to High School where she went to two different Chesterton Academies. In school she worked with accommodation and found her dream of publishing a book. Writing was difficult for her because of her Dyslexia and writing disorder, expressing herself was also a challenge since she has Autism. This book is her not letting those hardships hold her back and reaching for what seemed impossible.

Thank You to the Artists

Schafer, Kathelean.
Needle of Silver

Villegas, Savannah.
Mother By a Pond, Mustard Seed, Value

Laurenti, Peter.
Battle of the Leaf

Woolley, Angela.
Those Feet of Jesus, Sun Beam, Celebrate

Schade, Amelia.
Graveyards

Schafer, Richard.
Knot, Shoes

Thank you for the wonderful art work to go with the poems, your work brings life to the words.

www.ingramcontent.com/pod-product-compliance
Lightning Source LLC
Chambersburg PA
CBHW050114170426
43198CB00014B/2575